A WRITER'S GUIDE TO BREAKING BAD

Tony Conniff

Table of Contents

Foreword

I've read scores of books about screenwriting. Because the devices discussed herein are used every day by many good writers, it would be foolish to claim any 'secret knowledge'. But some of the techniques I found in Breaking Bad I've never seen described in any of those books.

I'm a professional musician, songwriter, screenwriter, writer. Not being formally schooled at any of these skills, the way I've learned, other than by doing them myself, is by studying people who did them well, in ways I liked, emulating (copying) them, and then absorbing their techniques into something of my own.

In addition to screenwriting, I'm a busy music producer, songwriter, and songwriting coach. For over 9 years I've written a weekly blog about songwriting that's built a worldwide readership and I've published a popular book for songwriters, 'Unpredictable Songwriting'.

As a bass player I studied the greats, such as James Jamerson, Chuck Rainey, Paul McCartney. As a songwriter I took apart songs I loved by the best songwriters from all eras and tried to figure out the underlying craft and techniques.

I try to understand how people whose work I admire 'think' about what they do, as they do it. (With playing music it's more of a prepared reflex in the moment than thought, but writing of course involves a lot of redoing and rewriting - thinking in a more traditional way).

When I watched Breaking Bad, and then watched it again, just for pleasure, I started to see patterns. But I couldn't yet place or describe exactly what the patterns were.

So, I decided to take a deep dive, as I had with music, songs, and movies, to attempt to better understand what was going on. Perhaps because of the narrow focus of Breaking Bad, I thought it might be comprehensible to me.

So, I watched it through several more times, taking notes... and I did start to see patterns. The writers seemed to have an approach, almost a set of 'rules', that they followed so consistently that it couldn't be an accident or coincidence. These approaches are what I've explored here.

I wrote this study for myself. I think it's helped me improve. I hope this short book will help some other writers, even experienced ones, get better too.

Character and Plot

It isn't easy to enmesh character and plot. It's uncommon to see it done well.

Often, we refer to dramas as 'story-driven' or 'character-driven', the former meaning a lot of plot with less character development and the latter meaning a study of character(s) with minimal story.

If you like a full serving of both at once... it can be pretty slim pickings. In Breaking Bad the story is character-driven, yet the characters seem to be lashed forward by an inexorable plot.

Anything with so much plot and suspense and so many thrills will never feel like a 'character piece', at least not at first. But Breaking Bad never disconnects from its characters to move the story forward or make it exciting. That's the key.

Breaking Bad didn't invent the wheel. There are few if any practices discussed here that aren't familiar to many writers and careful viewers. But Breaking Bad executed some of the truisms of dramatic writing to such a high degree, with such rigor and exuberance, that I felt sure it would repay a closer look.

"We just question everything. We thought of every possibility but then we had to vet it against, 'Is it legitimate against the character's forward momentum?'." - Vince Gilligan

In Breaking Bad, character is revealed by the pressures of the story. Not by explaining or having a weird quirk. And most of the story itself is created by the pressures inside the characters.

The characters are tested and exposed by conflicts that are not only intrinsic to the story, but as difficult as possible... and sometimes beyond.

Rarely is there the too-familiar feeling that a character is doing something they wouldn't do because the writers need them to. This is a flaw that eats away at the credibility of many dramatic works, no matter how enjoyable they may be in other ways.

If the Breaking Bad writers hadn't been so scrupulous about this they could have, as so many other dramatic works do, made choices resulting in short-term excitement at the cost of long- term credibility.

One can only imagine (actually you don't have to imagine; there are video interviews on YouTube) how difficult it was for the writers to stick with this demanding approach. Each time a character attempts to solve a problem in a way that's consistent with their personality, many, many other less consistent possibilities must be considered and rejected.

Another extraordinary aspect of Breaking Bad is its focus; how, over 62 hours, the writers explore the interlocking and shifting loyalties, conflicts, and betrayals between a literal handful of characters. One of the great benefits of this for the viewer (and challenges for the writers) is that almost everything that happens bears upon the main story and the main characters. There are *no digressions.*

Basically, it's about Walt and Skyler, Jesse, and Hank. Junior and Marie are important but rarely drive the main story's conflicts. Jane has a big impact but is around only briefly. There are the drug distributors: Gus is a major character for two seasons. Before him was Tuco; after him, Lydia. Mike and Saul are crucial but, again, they don't drive the story. They support it, as do other characters who come and go.

Almost everyone interacts with everyone else. One rarely feels that anything happens with a character in BB which is not relentlessly moving the story forward - especially by the end of Season 2.

There's a lot of discussion of character here, and I'll be looking at things from the writing perspective, so I'll note how hard it can be when watching the show to separate the writing from the casting choices, performances, and filmmaking.

For example, although Walter White as written is a fascinating, complex character, it's impossible to completely separate the writing from Bryan Cranston's skill. Walt travels the spectrum from super-nerd softie to ice-cold killer, often being at several places on the spectrum simultaneously, and Cranston makes it all believable. This kind of meshing is true of most of the actors and characters in this superbly cast and filmed show.

Now for the '10 Commandments' of Breaking Bad.

1

The Everyday Superpower

What makes Walt's story special and worth telling? He has a superpower - he's a brilliant chemist capable of making something that produces insane amounts of money - and he's willing and turns out to be able to use his 'superpower' beyond the boundaries of what's normally accepted, inside and outside the law. This makes his superpower dangerous for him and those around him (because it's profitable and illegal), and exciting for the viewer.

Walter White's Superpower is not only what makes him different, it's why there's a show.

This isn't an attempt to conflate a character like Walter White with Batman or Superman. It just means he's exceptional enough at something to make him interesting to the viewer and irreplaceable to the other characters... which offers a lot of story options and solutions.

It's important in this kind of story for a character to have a superpower. It doesn't have to put them in the Marvel Universe - think of Carrie Matheson or Guillame Debailly (espionage) or Mrs. Maisel (comedy)… and many others. Superpowers don't have to be caused by a meteor falling to earth, or an infection from a spider or a serum. They also don't have to be lethal.

The possibilities that their superpower awakens tests them by putting them in unusually complicated and risky situations from which their superpower has the potential to extricate them - if they can make the right decisions (fortunately for the stories, more often than not they don't).

As a superstar in the drug business Walt is worth hundreds of millions of dollars to his associates (and himself). This brings out the greed in almost everyone in the story, which motivates them.

But Walt finds that he not only wants his share of the money… he discovers that he wants everything - the power, the dominance, the validation - that his previous choices in life have denied him. When we meet Walter White all he does with his superpower is teach chemistry to disinterested high school students.

The writers don't overuse this, but when Walt's in a very tight spot, he jumps into a phone booth, turns from Clark Kent into Superman (Heisenberg), and utilizes his genius as a chemist, and eventually as a criminal, to get himself out of the jam.

Examples:

* Crazy 8 and cousin in the RV

* Blowing up Tuco's HQ

* Stealing methylamine using an Etch-A-Sketch

* Using household batteries to run an RV

* Eliminating his rivals to save his own life (Gus) or to get retribution (Lydia)

* Even, when he was just getting started, blowing up the expensive car of an annoying suit at a gas station

Walt's not invulnerable, but his chemistry powers, combined with his ruthlessness and his willingness to take risks, give him a crucial advantage.

Superpower (genius chemist)

+ calculated recklessness/risk-taking

+ ruthlessness/amorality

+ <u>instinct for finding others' weak spot</u>

= Walt's leverage

Also, Walt, Gus, and to some extent Hank, in their areas of power, can all see around the next corner. They have a 6th sense, an instinct for survival in the jungle. They smell the dangers and the opportunities before others can.

This leads to two other aspects that seem essential to sustaining interest in the main character's story.

The Obsession. Walter White is obsessed. He can't stop; he just can't let it go. He couldn't explain it to you, but when it comes to his inner goals, what he has to prove (to himself, mostly), he can't control his drive.

This constantly raises the stakes. When mortally challenged… a non-obsessed person would just walk away. Is it really worth risking your life, your family, your freedom? Of course not... unless you're totally obsessed.

With this kind of character at the center - Walter White, Tony Soprano, Carrie Matheson, Guilliame Debailly, the various power-mad Game of Thrones folks - being pushed way beyond a 'normal' person's limits, a writer can keep throwing higher and wider obstacles in their way... because they just will not quit. And they (and the writers) have to dig deeper to find a way out which, as we'll see, usually creates a new obstacle.

The Obsession applies to films as well, but less so. There are some great films where the main character isn't obsessed. But I'd suggest that this is far less likely to work in a long-form drama.

The Journey. A series of grueling tests that pushes the character deeper into who they are, and away from who they thought they were. They may or may not gain knowledge of themselves... but *we* do.

I don't want to get into spoilers here (outside of Breaking Bad), but if you think about where any effective main character starts off, what they go through, and where they end up... it's a long, strange trip.

Walter White starts as a milquetoast suburban high school teacher and ends up a savage, murderous, drug lord who destroys everything in his path plus, eventually, himself.

How did he get there?

The show started with the idea of a chemistry teacher who becomes a meth cook/drug dealer. But the writers pushed and pushed him until he broke everything around him, and then himself.

2

'Where's the character's head at?'

Vince Gilligan famously said, *"I ask myself, where's the character's head at?"*. This is one of BB's trademarks. It's amazing how often we writers *don't* ask ourselves this.

When relatively naive 'ordinary' people, like you and me and most in BB, witness or participate in shocking events, we're traumatized, and our reactions can be extreme. In BB, traumatic events happen constantly.

The characters don't pop up in the next scene or episode acting as if nothing happened (though they might be *pretending* that nothing happened). With emotion, or with suppressed emotion, they act… or act out. *The characters, like real people, never just 'move on', internally anyway.*

For example, in the Season (4)-long showdown between Walt and Gus, after Gus slashes Victor's throat just a few feet away from them (in the first episode), Walter buys a gun, Jesse self-medicates.

Walt and Jesse's shock at this event - where Gus intentionally reveals his utter ruthlessness and willingness to kill - reverberates and informs their actions through the entire season. Like most of us, when their lives are threatened with imminent violent death… it never just slips their mind.

Walt reacts as he usually does, at first - emotionally. He heads to Gus's house with the gun. (See 'First Try Never Works').

Walt's erratic actions in Season 4 are *always* informed by his panic at knowing that his life is in imminent danger - that Gus is working tirelessly to make him dispensable... so he can be eliminated.

As a counter-example, using a physical trauma, in a popular current show, a pretty good one, the lead character gets a few of his toenails ripped off and continues on as if nothing happened - no limp, no nothing. Whether the viewer is immediately conscious of it or not, this undermines narrative credibility — trust.

In BB, the characters almost never feel like they're doing things because the writers need or want them to. Their next movement of the plot is caused or affected by 'where the character's head's at'. And that reaction offers another opportunity to show us who they are.

This offers a double challenge to writer(s). (1) The 'next thing' has to make sense within the larger arc of the story and - especially since the show moves mostly chronologically, within the time frame of a year - (2) it has to feel created by something a character would actually do *in that moment, given what they've just been through.*

Angry Walt's initial response is always emotional and initially self-destructive (until he moves on to self-preservation by destroying someone else). Sensitive Jesse is usually on the verge of cracking up when something stressful happens. Skyler keeps it inside at first; then acts. Gus, the strategic thinker, suppresses his emotion (or is so used to doing so that he barely feels it anymore). Hank reacts by acting, charging the situation head-on. Oversimplified, but you get the idea.

Also, the characters don't just react emotionally, they *act out...* like real people.

Walt reacts to watching Tuco beat someone to death by coming home and forcing himself on his pregnant wife.

9

When Walt tries to force Skyler into making a decision about their future... she reacts by fucking Ted... and then throwing it in Walt's face. Walt reacts to this by going to Ted's office and trying to attack him.

When, in Ep. 16, Walt gets a bad cancer prognosis, then spends a few nightmarish days out in the desert cooking with Jesse, only to return to hear that his cancer is showing 'signs of remission'... He reacts in a counter-intuitive but true-to-his-character way by punching out a bathroom towel dispenser.

Hank's reactions are physical - he gets violent. When he's terrified of going to El Paso... he reacts by instigating an uncalled-for bar fight and beating on some druggy bikers (affirming his 'masculinity').

After Hank is 6 feet away from 'Heisenberg' (and Jesse) and is fooled into leaving, he goes to Jesse's house and gives him a vicious beating that jeopardizes Hank's own career.

Walt blows up a car... drives recklessly after Gus makes him a financial offer he can't refuse but knows he should... smashes a paper towel dispenser... burns money... gives a baffling talk at a school assembly after the plane crash... when stopped for a broken windshield gets himself pepper-sprayed and arrested... makes a big scene at Ted's office after

Skyler tells Walt she slept with him… then makes a pass at the principal of the school…

He does all of these stupid things immediately after something highly stressful occurs in his life.

3

Choosing Between Two Bad Options

You're writing Season 5 of Breaking Bad. Gus is dead. You want to put Mike in business with Walt and Jesse. How do you do it?

Mike is smart, savvy, and has highly developed survival skills. So, he knows that going into business with Walt, who he doesn't like or respect, and with whom he's been in constant conflict, is a bad idea. To put it mildly.

Mike sees Walt clearly: other than money, Walt will bring him nothing but trouble, which to Mike isn't worth the money. So why would Mike work with him?

You could have him just agree to do it because it's convenient for you, the writer. Walt and Jesse could talk him into it "against his better judgement".

You could have Walt offer to make him rich beyond his wildest dreams.

The character Mike as we've come to know him would never agree with any of these options - he likes money but he's not greedy. And he likes living more than money. Plus, it offends his sensibilities and professional pride to work with amateurs like Walt and Jesse.

He finally agrees because he's faced with only two choices - bad and worse.

The government seizes his assets, leaving him without money for his granddaughter's care after he's gone. His crew has been arrested and their money has also been seized. It's almost certain that at least one of them will flip and put Mike in prison for the rest of his life. That's option one.

The other alternative, that *might* solve this problem? Go into business with someone he not only despises and doesn't trust, but who he believes is almost guaranteed to come to a bad end. But as bad as this is for Mike… it's still better than the alternative.

This is classic Breaking Bad.

In most dramas, the very common situation of having one character trying to get another to do something they don't want to do is handled, broadly speaking, in one of three ways.

1) Ask 'Pretty please'.

Usually, they say No at first. Then they're asked again with a little more emphasis; either a verbal or physical push or a shove, some mild incentive, or... 'Come on... Pretty please? I'll be your best friend...'

By far the most common, and by far the least satisfying.

2) Make it physically hard.

A chase, a fight, a car crash, etc.

Better... but most of the time all this tells us is that the character cares enough to run up a hill, get into a fist fight, or risk something, in some way.

3) Give them Two Bad Choices... and make them choose.

This is how BB does it. By far the best way.

Why? Because the character's choice of actions can reveal so much about who they are. And, since their choice often reveals that they're not who they think or say they are (not the case with Mike), we also see the gap between how they see themselves and who they really are.

A tough choice reveals character. A virtually impossible choice can reveal character deeply.

Breaking Bad constantly forces its characters to make choices that are as close to impossible - two terrible alternatives - as they can be.

Examples:

*   At the beginning and for some time Walt and Jesse work together because their other options are worse (over time they get caught up in their own dysfunctional spiral which often - but not always - supersedes necessity.)

*   Walt has one hour to find and deliver his meth to Gus or lose 15 million dollars and his distribution opportunity... just when his wife is about to give birth and he needs to be at the hospital *now*. He delivers the meth and misses the birth. That's Walt.

*   Jesse falls in junkie love with Jane, a manipulative drug addict. She forces him to choose between her and Walt... He chooses her... which leads to...

Walt sees Jane overdosing. He can help her... but her survival is a major long-term problem for him; she's a grave threat to his whole operation... and she definitely threatens his bizarre bond with Jesse. Or he can choose to *not* help her... and she'll die choking on her own vomit. For most of us, this wouldn't be much of a choice. For Walt...

The writers could have resolved 'the Jane problem' many different ways. It's telling that they chose to do it in a way that starts with Jesse's 'two bad options' - Walt or Jane? - and then gives Walt, their main character, a fork in the road which is arguably the tipping point that sends him irrevocably to the dark side.

* Jesse shoots Gale when he has a choice - he and Walt will die... or he can kill Gale, at least buying them some time. Kill or be killed.

* Hank is a few feet from Heisenberg (Walt) - his prey, his obsession, his Moby Dick - when he's told that his wife Marie is in the hospital. He immediately leaves to be with her. That's Hank.

* In Season 5, Hank can finally bring down Heisenberg (Walt), but it will definitely cost him his job and his career... which, other than Marie (and getting

Heisenberg), is all that matters to him. He goes after Heisenberg.

By having Hank, at moments of high stress where split-second choices are made not by thought but by instinct, make choices between what are to him two impossible options we see what *really* matters to Hank, who he *really* is.

And we get to see what a basically good man like Hank does - including dying not with panic and fear but as a hero - contrasted with what a bad man, a lost soul (Walter) does at similar moments of stress.

* Walt, expert at manipulating Jesse, sees him getting close to Andrea and Brock, which will create a weak spot for his enterprise. Instead of directly advising Jesse to let go of them, which is what Walt wants, he advises the opposite - tell her everything - correctly believing that Jesse, at heart a decent person who would never put a child in danger, will *not* tell Andrea everything, but rather leave them.

This isn't exactly the kind of choice we've been discussing. Jesse doesn't have 'a gun to his head', as BB characters often do. But he could have selfishly held on to Andrea and Brock, putting their lives in jeopardy - as Walter does with his family - or he could let

17

go of them... which is what he chooses to do. Two bad options.

This choice tells us who Jesse is at heart. It also again contrasts with Walt, who is always on the lookout for his associates' weak spots - that is, their humanity - so he can use them to his advantage.

* Hector loathes Walt - he considers Walt responsible for the death of relatives he loved - and under normal circumstances would never consider working with him. (In fact, Hector would certainly kill Walt if he was not paralyzed and physically incapable of doing so.)

But... Hector hates Gus even more. So, when Walt comes to him with a plan to finish off Gus, Hector has to make a life and death decision and he chooses the lesser - to him - of two evils. Or the greater of two satisfying revenges... which he gives his own life to achieve... leaving Walt hubristically triumphant in victory.

4

First Try Never Works

And if and when it finally works... it usually creates a new, often worse, problem.

Often the 'tries' are attempts to find a weak spot. Like in a chess game, the adversaries probe, fail, pull back, try another approach, until they find the vulnerability in their opponent's position. Almost anything tried by a character in Breaking Bad fails at least once, if not (as in Walt and Gus's cat-and-mouse game) many times. *Nothing is easy.*

'First try never works' is a narrative strategy that, although it really kicks in with Season 3, is so prevalent throughout the show (with the notable exception of Season 5), sometimes through very long arcs, that I'll only cite a few examples.

* Walt cooks the best meth in the world

He and Jesse try to distribute it themselves

After Combo (dealing) is shot dead by a child on a street corner...

They accept that it's not going to work

Saul sets up a meet with Gus

Jesse shows up high

Gus doesn't even come out

(Saul: 'He's cautious. It's over.')

Walt doesn't give up. He goes back to Gus's restaurant - alone

He waits a long time for Gus, who finally talks to him

Gus knows Jesse was high and doesn't deal with addicts

Walt says his product is the best, he has 38 lbs. of it, and Gus will never see Jesse

Gus takes his number

On another day, Gus's man tells Walt he has one hour to deliver the drugs

And if he misses the deadline, 'Don't show your face'

Missing the birth of his child, Walt gets it there on time

This solution to his money problem, his find-a-distributor problem, creates a worse problem:

Walt now works for Gus

* Gomie indulges Hank and searches the laundry for a meth lab with police dogs

The lab is actually there, in the basement, but Gomie finds nothing

* Walt and Jesse are prisoners of meth-crazed Tuco and his Uncle Hector in an isolated house

Jesse tells Tuco the meth has chili powder (thinking he'll like it because he's Mexican)

Tuco: 'I hate chili powder.'

So, Walt puts deadly ricin in Tuco's burrito

In an unrelated rage, Tuco knocks all the food off the table

Finally, while Jesse and Tuco scuffle, Walt gets Tuco's gun and shoots him

* Jesse's parents kick him out of where he's living

He has no place to live now

He hits up an old friend... who takes him in...

Until his wife makes Jesse leave

Jesse sneaks into his RV

The tow guy kicks him out of the yard

He steals the RV and drives it away through the gate

To Walt's house (a new problem)

* Hank turns down a promotion to El Paso and stays in Albuquerque to find the RV

They track down all 29 RVs in the area

He stakes out the final RV. He's sure this one is it

The RV belongs to an old couple and Hank embarrasses himself surveilling it

He's told in the office that they've checked all the RVs

He asks them to look one more time

There's one more RV out there (*That was easy!* This is one of the few easy turnarounds in all of Breaking Bad)

Hank goes to the address where it's registered

Combo's Mom lives there

On the wall of Combo's room, he sees a picture of Combo and Jesse - Bingo!

5

The Weak Spot

A character's weak spot is what makes them relatable, sympathetic, understandable. It's usually their family, or those they love. It's what makes them like the rest of us - human.

It's also where their vulnerability is. For that reason, it's their weak spot. It's where they can be 'gotten'. It's their Kryptonite. When someone ruthless wants something, a character's weak spot is their leverage. And Walter White is a stone-cold-heartless weak-spot-finding genius.

Other than Jane, Jesse's weak spot is children. Still a lost child himself, an innocent who's been corrupted by the 'adults' around him, for Jesse protecting a child trumps anything else he may want or be forced to do.

When Jesse goes the house of a crackhead couple who stole his money, to kill them... there's a child there, which changes everything for him. When Brock's life is endangered Jesse tells the doctors about Ricin, which puts him directly in the sights of the police. When Todd shoots a kid on a bike, an innocent witness, Jesse becomes unhinged. When Andrea is killed by Todd near the end it's the threat that they will then kill her son Brock that keeps Jesse cooking meth (he'd rather die - in a moment of desperation he asks them to kill him - but saving Brock's life is more important).

And his biggest (downward) turning point is when he kills Gale... who is himself just another big kid.

Similarly, when Jesse is seducing Andrea with the goal of selling drugs to her, he doesn't know she has a son. When her son Brock comes home, it changes everything. As soon as he realizes Andrea has a child, he can't tolerate the idea of her using drugs.

The one time that Jesse really opens his heart, other than with children, is with Jane. This leads to her death. Between killing Gale and feeling responsible for Jane's death, Jesse becomes truly lost.

Hank's biggest weak spot is his love for his wife Marie. When Hank has Walt dead to rights, trapped in an RV with Jesse, with no way out... Walt, with his uncanny instinct for the weaknesses of others, fakes a call telling Hank that Marie is in the hospital.

Without hesitation Hank abandons his obsessive pursuit of Heisenberg to rush to Marie. (Contrast this with Walter's action when the birth of his baby coincides with an important drug deal).

Hank has another, similar weak spot for someone he also loves - Walt. He can't see what's right in front of his face.

Gus, Walt's greatest adversary, doesn't seem to have a weak spot. Unlike Walt, he has nerves of steel; he's controlled, disciplined, strategic, and flexible in the pursuit of his goals.

Except... for his hatred of Hector (which in flashbacks we see his good reasons for) and his need for revenge which, in true Gus style, is a dish he eats cold, over time. Finally, after much probing, Walt finds this weakness - that Gus, if provoked, would not be able to resist taking his revenge on Hector in person - and uses it to do in Gus.

(See 'The New Character' for a discussion of how, outside the main story, the *only* things we find out about BB's subsidiary characters relates to their Weak Spot... which then ends up connecting to the main story.)

6

Use Everything

Most long-form episodic shows, 6 hours or 62, look at the form as a way to put in 'character' material that in a tighter format would be cut. Most shows are just too long for the story they have to tell; they're padded with 'character' information and detail that's extraneous to the story.

The Breaking Bad writers turned the challenge of dealing with a very restricted cast of important characters into an asset. They used the limited forces at play to create even more conflict, and conflicts of interest.

Where most dramas add, say, a boyfriend or a girl-friend so we can see 'another side' of the character, in Breaking Bad if that new character didn't become essential to the main story as well, they weren't there.

And since Breaking Bad is a small world, rarely does anything happen where the effects don't ripple through other characters' lives.

Take Skyler's boyfriend Ted (please…). Ted could've just been an attractive guy who has an affair with his bookkeeper Skyler that affects her marriage. But he's also been cooking his books, which will implicate Skyler (and then Walt). So, she gives Ted the money for his 600K IRS bill… using the money that later Walt will need, and not have anymore, to save them.

Ted was there to give Skyler a release, to create conflict with Walt… but his financial problems and Skyler's complicity with them soon became essential to the main story.

As a bonus we saw Skyler, in trying to escape Walt, somehow get involved with another self- deceiving criminal with a whiny, wimpy side. People are like that.

There's Jesse's girlfriend Andrea (and son Brock). Andrea and Brock became important players in the unfolding of Jesse's fate in the story - not just his emotional life.

There are certain things that are planted in the story to be used and reused later - especially Walt's 'second cell phone' and the Ricin. But in finding answers to storytelling challenges of the moment, the writers looked back at the seeds they'd already planted, sometimes probably inadvertently, and used them.

"Look backwards instead of looking forward" - Peter Gould (Breaking Bad writer/producer) For example, Gould brought up, "Who's the other Chicken Brother?"

As I understand it, in trying to find more to work with for the Gus character, instead of just making up some completely new material, they characteristically looked back at what they already had.

Gus's company is Los Pollos Hermanos - The Chicken Brothers. Of course, that could just be a name, a brand. But what if there was another Chicken Brother...? Who was he? A partner of Gus's... What happened to him? How did it affect Gus?

This leads to the backstory of Gus's involvement with Don Elario and the cartel and Gus's Weak Spot (his hatred for and need for revenge on Hector) and became essential to how the story played out.

The philosophy seems to have been to waste as little as possible - characters, locations, physical objects.

7

Characters Compromised and Complicated

The small world of Breaking Bad demands that whenever possible characters should be both adversaries *and* allies and that each character should be as close and dependent on their adversary/ally as possible.

The show puts the characters directly in conflict with each other but needing to cooperate in some way (Walt and Gus) or puts them at odds because they have secrets and have to lie to each other - thereby compromising them and their relationship (Walt and Skyler... Walt and everyone).

In Breaking Bad, as often in life, it's money that compromises people. The writers use the enormous sums of money in the meth business to make virtually everyone compromised - and vulnerable. (Even, finally, Hank.)

There's also the excitement, for Walt and Hank especially. As James Ellroy put it, "Crime is a thrill."

(Compromises can work in other ways too. For example, love can make you compromise yourself and your deeply held personal/professional/moral principles, as in Homeland or The Bureau.)

The compromise is gradual. You need the money... so you make the accommodation and accept what comes with it. This is true for most of us in everyday life.

But in the far more extreme world of Breaking Bad many of the characters, when brought up to a line they thought they could never cross... cross it and become *deeply* compromised and vulnerable. Also, when you accept someone with whom you're intimate, and *they* are compromised... you become compromised too.

For example, Skyler, initially just trying to keep her family together, slowly gets pulled in by Walter's meth money, and eventually becomes an active participant in the criminal enterprise. In the end she 'gets away with it' (with Walt's help) but is shattered; her family and her idea of who she is irreparably broken.

Hank and Marie are the last to be compromised. Hank is not corruptible by money, but Marie takes Walt and Skyler's money for Hank's medical bills (anyone in America can understand why she did this). Because she knows Hank's pride would not allow it - and she doesn't know the money is illegal - Marie doesn't tell Hank. In the endgame, with Skyler's help, Walt exploits this.

Also, Marie doesn't tell Hank about the money until she has to, which is understandable given his character, her love for him, that she trusts Skyler, and of course, Hank and Walt's close 'friendship'. As a result, even Hank and Marie's solid relationship is threatened when she lies to him about something that turns out to be life-altering.

In Breaking Bad, money is the root of all the evil. The desire for money and the power that comes with it - greed, survival, dominance - is the primary motivation of most of the characters.

8

BUT ALSO

The characters are in conflict with themselves - or if they're not when we meet them, the pressures of the story bring out their internal conflicts.

Walt is an underachieving nerd who loves his family, wants to be liked, and wants to 'do the right thing' BUT ALSO he's a ruthless, reckless drug dealer and murderer.

Jesse is an ignoramus drug addict and dealer BUT ALSO he's a sensitive and artistic soul.

Walt is manipulative and constantly abusive to Jesse BUT ALSO Jesse's the only one to whom Walt is loyal and to whom he shows his true self.

Skyler is a strong, family-oriented soccer mom BUT ALSO allows herself to be seduced by money and power.

To Walt, Hank is a paradigm of masculinity and loyalty BUT ALSO Walt's biggest threat.

Marie gives Hank love and maternal caring BUT ALSO makes him feel the vulnerability beneath his hyper-masculinity... which he hates.

Hank makes Marie feel safe and secure BUT ALSO in his line of work he could be killed at any time.

Saul is weak, amoral, and criminal BUT ALSO underneath he's a decent softie who gives good advice (almost always ignored).

Jane brings to Jesse love, intimacy, and vulnerability (his artistic side) BUT ALSO moves Jesse deeper into addiction and danger.

(Walt and Jesse are afraid of who they really are - they've spent their lives up to this point pretending to be the *opposite*. As Vince Gilligan put it, *"Walter White seems like the antithesis of a criminal when we first meet him. He really was meant to be a criminal. Jesse Pinkman, who when we meet him is a criminal, should never have been a criminal."*)

Walt is a family man BUT ALSO a criminal. (Gus seems to be this as well - we don't see his family, but he presents himself as a family man).

Jesse is a junkie BUT ALSO responsible (when clean).

Hank is a courageous hero BUT ALSO a coward.

Inner conflict and outer compromise; the hallmarks of most Breaking Bad characters.

9

Family Ties

Though they can be complicated (which is dramatically good), bonds between family members usually don't need as much explanation or justification as other connections. Involving family members has the uncommon benefit of making some things easier for the writer while still remaining hard for the characters.

Why does Skyler stand for it? Well, she and Walt have been together for 20 years. They have two children together. Everyone understands these bonds.

Family ties also give the characters built-in Weak Spots - they can be compromised by threats to the people they love.

Walt - Skyler, Walt junior, and Holly, as well as in-laws Hank and Marie - they're all family. When Gus turns the ultimate screws on Walt, he threatens to kill Walt's family. When Walt finally gives in and gives up, in the penultimate episode, he's trying to save Hank's life.

As much as he abuses their love and trust and takes them for granted, to the very end Walt never stops caring about his family, albeit in a thoroughly narcissistic way. This plays a significant part in retaining some sympathy for him ('He's not *all* bad...').

Like Michael Corleone, he rationalizes his crimes by telling himself he's 'doing it for my family'.

Jesse - Jesse's lack of family defines his lost, childlike character and his need for other, family-like (especially father-figure) connections.

His early disconnection from his parents lends credibility to his dependence on Walt (and his susceptibility to being repeatedly exploited by him), and later to Gus. He latches onto Jane like a drowning man, or a lost child finding his mother.

Later, Andrea and Brock become a surrogate family for Jesse. He loves them enough to let go of them when he understands that their lives will be tainted and threatened by his work. (Contrast with Walt who, even when he's manipulating Jesse into giving up Andrea, is able to convince himself that he, Walt, can 'have it all' - his life of crime, his fortune, *and* a safe, unscathed family.)

Skyler - Along with Walt, Junior, and Holly, there's her sister Marie and brother-in-law Hank.

Hector - Tuco is his nephew. Because he holds Walt responsible for Tuco's death, his desire for revenge hangs over Walt's head.

Tuco - When his cousins come to America for revenge, they won't stop until they kill his killer (Walt). As thousands of dramas have shown (along with real life), seeking revenge for hurting or killing a relative requires little or no explanation.

Andrea - She lost her brother to the streets; now she wants to protect her son Brock. She becomes a victim due to her surrogate family relationship with Jesse. She and her son become his Weak Spot.

Mike - His daughter-in-law and, most crucially, his granddaughter (his dead son's wife and daughter) are his main motivation. We need to be told very little about why they're so important to him.

Jane - When Jane dies of an overdose her father goes off the rails, with catastrophic consequences. We see how invested he is in Jane and her sobriety. Since Jane is his daughter there's no need to ask why.

<u>Gus</u> mentions his family, but they're never shown, making him a single-minded foe to Walt, without a family weak spot.

10

The New Character

The new character added to Breaking Bad must provide an essential function - helping the story expand organically - *and* be interesting in and of themself. The key is integrating these two aspects.

Many of these characters can also be seen as contrasts - shadows - to other characters. Hank and Gus are this for Walt, in different ways.

Beyond what's necessary for a new character's direct utility in moving the story forward, we are only given just enough of their personal life *to show their Weak Spot* - the part of their life that will make them vulnerable within the story. *The rest of their life is left out.*

(Also see 'Family Ties')

Gus

Function

First, he replaces Tuco as Walt's distributor. He quickly becomes Walt's boss.

Gus is so disciplined that he can hide in plain sight as a respected legitimate businessman, community leader, and even an active backer of local DEA and law enforcement. He plays this role with apparent sincerity and commitment, not only contributing time and money to good causes but even humbly busing tables at his chain of restaurants. Outwardly he's the model of a self-made honest and successful businessman - a perfect cover.

He's there to be Walt's antagonist. Only one of them can be left standing and, for most of Gus's time on the show, it looks like it will be Gus. He has so much more going for him than Walt, who is *way* out of his league against Gus.

It's a great example of overmatching your main character, your hero or anti-hero. The antagonist (Gus, in this case) is so clearly superior that the protagonist (Walt) is beaten at every turn and must dig deeper than they ever have, must find resources (and depths) that they never knew they had, to triumph in the end.

The antagonist pushes the main character into discovering who they really are and what they never would have known about themself if, in order to survive, they weren't tested to a seemingly impossible degree.

Personality

Gus is the opposite of his predecessor, the demented drug addict/dealer Tuco and, in another way, of slightly less demented Walt (who at least doesn't use his own product). Gus is rational and tightly controlled where Walt is emotional and hot-headed. Gus sees the big picture. He always plans many moves ahead.

We don't see any side of Gus that doesn't apply to the story. He speaks of family, but when Walt and Jesse visit his home, we don't see them. He's a 'pure' antagonist for Walt (and Hank). Other than a few crucial flashbacks to Mexico and current visits to Hector (used to show what will emerge as his Weak Spot), almost all we know about Gus is what Walt, Jesse, Mike, and Hank see when they're with him.

Saul

Function

When Walter needs anything, sleazy attorney Saul always 'knows a guy'. This allows Walt to get beyond his suburban vanilla frame of reference and into the world of shady (and worse) characters.

This is tremendously helpful to the storytelling. Walt - and the writers - have a problem to solve? Saul 'knows a guy'. Very useful to have someone like this around if you're an inexperienced aspiring criminal (or writing about one).

Even better for this long story, Saul's guys not only solve problems for Walt, but they also present new ones (Gus being the prime example).

Personality

Saul is sleazy, but he has a strong strain of decency. He can suggest that Walt and Jesse kill Badger and in the next breath express sincere concern for Walt's health.

The first advice he gives Walt is often good. He attempts to deflect Walt from his path of destruction, self- and otherwise. But Walt always ignores this counsel and demands what he needs to further his dark ambitions.

So even though Saul tries (and wants, really) to do right, he's easily pushed back on - he's weak and he's greedy. The power of Walt's money and domineering personality is too much for Saul to resist.

Mike

Function

Mike is Gus's 'muscle' and 'chief of intelligence'. He's smart and experienced. Gus, who trusts no one, depends on him.

Walt's charm is lost on Mike, thereby creating conflict, because a big part of Mike's job turns out to be saving Walt's ass. They ultimately become partners… which doesn't end well. Mike knew it wouldn't but… (see 'Choosing Between Two Bad Options').

Personality

Mike is a Clint Eastwood-type character - so good at what he does, such a badass, so self-contained within his own moral code, so tough (and ruthless), that it's hard not to admire him, to think he's cool.

He also adores his granddaughter and takes loving care of her and her Mom. It's his Weak Spot, but it gives him a higher purpose and, as is often the case, makes us see his human side and like him more.

__Gale__

Function

Gale replaces Jesse as Walt's assistant in the lab. Educated and a rare talent at chemistry himself, he recognizes and understands Walt's genius as a chemist in a way no one else does. He's a libertarian, which gives him a rationale for his involvement with drugs.

He's actually a perfect assistant for Walt... the old Walt, that is. The nerdy schoolteacher chemist Walt. The new Walt needs Jesse. And, since Gus has slated Gale to replace Walt... Gale, from Walt's angle, has a target on his back.

Personality

A sweet guy who somehow ended up on the dark side. An uber-nerd, a nerd of nerds. Like 'The 40-Year-Old Virgin', his apartment is filled with models he's built or collected. He's child-like and adoring of Walt and his skills. His initial scenes in the lab with Walt are basically 'nerds fall in love' scenes.

Jane

Function

A unique character in the show, Jane is around only briefly (Season 2, Episodes 4-12 - and she's not even in all of them). But she has an enormous impact on the characters she interacts with and on the story. First of all, on Jesse, who falls in love with her and remains guilt-ridden and haunted by her for as long as we know him.

Along with turning Jesse from a druggie into a real junkie, she touches and wakes up parts of Jesse that have been asleep. Not only his ability to care for someone else, but the part of him that's creative, an artist. Through Jane's influence, Jesse becomes and remains a much more sensitive and empathetic person.

Because of Jane, Jesse begins to experience that there's something else you can do with feelings other than push them away with drugs (though he and Jane do plenty of that too). The interplay between Jesse's increased capacity to feel and the horrible things he will do and endure deepens the rest of his journey, much to the benefit of the story. Jane is the instigator of this.

Jesse's never the same after she dies. This is Jane's most important 'function' - she opens Jesse's heart, but she also pushes Jesse and Walt to another level. Deeper - and lower.

Jane's control over Jesse, which threatens Walt's, leads Walt to take another step on his road to murder - he becomes a passive murderer. He lets Jane die. He watches her die. A giant step on Walt's path to complete perdition - not only making and selling lethal drugs, but ultimately becoming a mass murderer.

The grief and guilt Jane's air traffic controller father feels after her death leads him to negligently allow a plane crash to happen over Albuquerque. This tragedy affects all the characters.

Personality

Although the character as played by Kristen Ritter is vivid, in her brief time we find out very little about her other than how she relates to Jesse and her father. She's an addict who's sober... but she allows Jesse, a drug dealer using a fake name ('Jesse Jackson') to rent the apartment next door - a questionable move for someone supposedly committed to maintaining her sobriety.

Unlike Jesse, she has a willful and manipulative personality. She cares about him, but once she's back on drugs she's a classic scheming, devious addict. She lies to her father about her sobriety. Her greed and control of Jesse put the two of them in mortal conflict with Walt (and she understandably has no idea how ruthless an adversary she's taken on).

Todd

Function

Initially Todd fills Jesse's shoes as Walt's assistant when Walt and Jesse split, post-Gus. He comes from, and is closely attached to, a family gang of criminals. This both gives him backup (Walt has to consider this when dealing with Todd; it limits his options) and allows the writers to bring in those criminals - Todd's Uncle Jack and his gang of Neo-Nazis - as a major factor in Season 5. (See 'Use Everything'. They weren't going to waste Todd's crime family.)

Personality

Todd is easygoing, gentle even. Unlike Jesse, he's not tortured by his choices and the damage he's done. He's a nice young man with good manners who's troubled when he inconveniences people. Unlike his family gang, he doesn't enjoy hurting or killing anyone and tries to avoid it when he can.

He's also an amoral sociopath without a conscience who, when he sees it as a necessity, can murder a child without a second thought.

He apologizes when he or his accomplices hurt or kill someone, but he doesn't lose any sleep over it. He has no judgement about murder and extreme cruelty. That's just the way it is; for him it's just part of everyday life. (It's terrifying to imagine Todd's childhood.)

His crush on Lydia humanizes him a bit, but even if Lydia reciprocated, it never feels like Todd has the humanity to actually connect with another person (like Jesse does with Jane), even another psycho like Lydia, in the unlikely event that she'd be interested.

Lydia

Function

The show needed someone like Lydia in Season 5. With Gus gone, how would distribution-challenged Walt and Jesse make the amount of money needed to raise the stakes for the show's climax?

Lydia's monstrous and amoral greed is a driver for the season. She has the distribution; she opens new markets for the Walt and his partners - international, not local - and she has access to methylamine, the difficult-to-get but necessary element in cooking potent meth. Her distribution brings them riches beyond their wildest imaginings - along with the deadly problems that go with that much illegal money.

Personality

Unfortunately, other than having a child she truly loves (her Weak Spot, along with her greed), Lydia lacks dimension. She stays on one note, or at most one chord, all the time - high-strung and anxious, avaricious, and amoral, without conscience or scruples. In having so few registers, she's unique among the important characters on the show.

Afterword

I hope you've enjoyed this exploration of Breaking Bad and gotten some useable ideas from it. I'd love to hear from you if you have any thoughts, comments, additions, or disagreements… write to me through my website (tonyconniff.com).

I'd appreciate it if you'd pass this on to other writers. It's easy (and inexpensive) to get this book, in various formats, on my website or at Amazon.com. Thanks!

Acknowledgements

Special thanks to Chris Gerolmo, Alexa Junge, and Kevin Wade, and also to Dr. Michael Tanner and Peter Kleinhans, for reading various parts and iterations of this book and offering their thoughts, encouragement, and counsel. Any sloppy thinking, infelicitous prose, or errors of judgement that remain are all mine.

Thanks to Pooja Mehra for excellent formatting work and much appreciation for Jana Jelovac's cover design.

To DS Sulaitis for love, kindness, encouragement, inspiration, and a lot more.

And, always, to Emma Conniff and Asher Conniff, and to their mom, Aimee Greenstein.

About the Author

Tony Conniff is a recording artist, writer, songwriter, producer/mixer, musician, and teacher based in New York City. His albums, 'Let It Drown Me' (2017), 'Tight Leash' (2019), and 'Somehow We Survived (2021) are available on his website and on all digital platforms.

His bestselling book, 'Unpredictable Songwriting', is available in paperback, Kindle, and ebook formats on his website and at Amazon.com.

His bi-weekly Songwriting Blog has a worldwide readership. There are over 400 blogposts, about all aspects of songwriting, available free on his website (you can sign up there to receive new ones).

Feel free to contact Tony directly through his website regarding his scripts, as well as individual coaching and recording/production/mixing. You can also listen to his songs and productions there and sign up to receive writing-related updates and information about his publications, events, and workshops. www.tonyconniff.com

Made in the USA
Las Vegas, NV
06 May 2024

89610478R00037